Toads and their young

Colin S Milkins and Bobbie Neate

Read some chapters and then compare this animal with a robin, a stickleback, a grass snake, a rabbit or a dragonfly.

Contents

What is a toad?

A toad is an amphibian.

Amphibians are a group of animals that have backbones and are cold blooded. They can live on land or in water but they lay their eggs in water. Amphibians do not have scales like fish and reptiles.

⬆ Toads have a soft, loose, moist skin.

There are many kinds of amphibians. Frogs, newts and salamanders are all amphibians.

A newt.

A salamander.

The scientific name for a toad is Bufo bufo.

Where a toad lives

A toad lives on land most of the time.

⬆ Toads like to hide in long grass.

A toad likes to live under a stone or log. It comes out at night to find its food.

🔺 Toads do not always live in water.

A toad only spends four weeks in water, this is when it lays its eggs. The rest of the time it stays on dry land.

🔺 A toad hibernates in the winter under logs or stones.

What a toad eats

A toad eats insects, flies, ants, spiders, caterpillars, woodlice and worms.

⬆ Toads eat live insects.

🔺 A toad traps its food by shooting out its long, sticky tongue.

A toad swallows the insects it catches whole. Toads do not have teeth so they do not chew their food.

The insects it wants to catch must be alive and moving. If an insect stops moving the toad will not try to catch it.

Enemies

Young toads and the tadpoles are eaten by snakes, magpies and blackbirds.

⬆ The toad is trying to frighten its enemy.

Adult toads are eaten by birds such as magpies and crows. The birds only eat the inside of the toad as the skin is poisonous. Rats, grass snakes and hedgehogs eat toads. They eat the whole toad.

Defending itself

A toad escapes from its enemies by puffing itself up to make itself look really big. This can frighten the enemy away.

The toad is poisonous. It has little glands on its back. These look like little spots. If the glands are bitten they taste horrible to many animals.

Home of the young

Toads lay their eggs in ponds.

The place where the eggs are laid does
not have a special name.

⬆ The female toad carefully chooses shallow water to lay her
eggs. Shallow water is warmer than deep water.

Toads always lay their eggs in the pond where they were born.

Sometimes adult toads walk a long way to find the pond where they were born. Toads find their way back to their pond by following a smell. Each pond has a different smell.

The eggs

The female toad lays a long line of eggs called spawn.

⬆ The female lays her eggs around plants so that they do not get pulled away and fall into deep water.

Each black egg has clear jelly around it. This string of spawn can be very long.

The eggs are very small, only 2 millimetres.

Egg laying

The female toad lays her unfertilised eggs in water and the male toad puts his sperm on top of the eggs.

When the male lays his sperm on top of the female's eggs the eggs are fertilised. These eggs can now start to develop into toads.

The female toad can lay up to 4,000 eggs.

Care of the eggs

The eggs are not looked after by the male or female toad after they have been laid.

Protection of the eggs

The female toad does not protect her eggs after she has laid them.

↑ A pond with weeds is a good place to lay eggs.

The female's job is to find the best place to lay the eggs so that lots of them will live.

Hatching

It takes about 11 days before the tadpoles inside the eggs are ready to hatch.

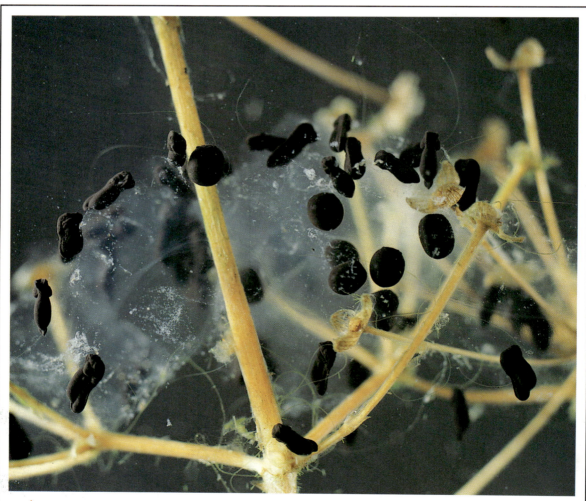

⬆ The tadpole inside the egg gets bigger and bigger until it is strong enough to swim away from the jelly.

Young toads

The very young toad does not look like its parents. It looks like a small fish. The very young toad is called a tadpole.

⬆ Tadpoles.

At first the tadpole can do nothing but eat the jelly from its egg but as it gets bigger it can swim and find food. After about 12 days the young tadpole likes to eat animal food. It will eat other tadpoles if they are dead.

↑ After five weeks the tadpole grows legs.

🔺 A toadlet looks like a very small, adult toad.

After 12 weeks the arms appear and the tails grow smaller and disappear. Now it is called a toadlet.

Care of the young

Toads do not look after their young. The tadpoles and toadlets look after themselves.

⬆ Toadlets catch food with their sticky tongues.

Tadpoles and toadlets have to catch their own food. Toadlets catch small flies, ants and other insects.

Becoming adults

It takes three or four years before a toadlet becomes the size of an adult toad.

Having their own families

After three or four years a toad can start to have its own family in the pond where it was born.

Some toads live a long time. Some toads have lived as long as 40 years.

Glossary of words used in this book

Backbone   The backbone is the line of bones of an animal's back.

Clear   Clear is when you can see through something.

Cold blooded   Cold blooded animals have the same temperature as their surroundings.

Glands   Glands are an important part of an animal's body. They help it stay healthy. They can also produce poisons.

Hatch   To hatch is when the animal inside an egg breaks out.

Jelly   Jelly is the outside of an egg. It is the part the tadpoles eat after they have hatched.

Scientific name   A scientific name is the name given to plants and animals by scientists.

Shallow   Shallow water is not deep. Shallow water is warmer than deep water.

Spawn   Spawn is the group of eggs laid by the female.

Sperm   Sperm is made by male animals. Eggs cannot develop without sperm.

Tadpole   A tadpole is the animal that has hatched out of the egg. It looks more like a fish than a toad.

Toadlet   A toadlet is a baby toad. It was a tadpole but now it has lost its tail and has grown legs and arms.

Unfertilised   Unfertilised means the eggs will not hatch out unless the male puts sperm on them.

Index

a b c d e f g h i j k l m n o p q r s t u v w x y z
A B C D E F G H I J K L M N O P Q R S T U V W X Y Z